A dedicated minimalist and accidental humorist, Neil lives with his partner, Helen, and their two pugs, Billy and Bella. His career path resembles a patchwork quilt, varied and interesting; travelling extensively; meeting incredibly fascinating and also prosaic people along the way. Previously a guitarist and songwriter in his spare time, he took up motorcycling in 2001, the freedom of which keeps him sane in an increasingly insane world. He turned to writing in 2015 and is busy writing a second book in his *Ultimate* series, with a third bubbling enthusiastically on the back burner.

Ali
Health & happiness.
always.
Neil

Dedication

Donald Law 12/10/1931 – 06/02/2015
A true gentleman.

Neil D. Law

MOTORCYCLING:
THE ULTIMATE THERAPY

AUSTIN MACAULEY PUBLISHERS™

LONDON • CAMBRIDGE • NEW YORK • SHARJAH

A CIP catalogue record for this title is available from the British Library.

ISBN 9781788483537 (Paperback)
ISBN 9781788483544 (Hardback)
ISBN 9781788483551 (E-Book)

www.austinmacauley.com

First Published (2018)
Austin Macauley Publishers Ltd™
25 Canada Square
Canary Wharf
London
E14 5LQ

Acknowledgments

My irrepressible mum, Brenda, and my sibling jewels, Malcolm, Andrew and Carolyn. Thank you for all the fun, happiness, love and merciless teasing we share.

My partner, Helen – Thank you for your devotion, love and support throughout, convincing me every day that all this was a good idea.

John, Sylvia, Liam, Eddie, Alison and Tont – For allowing me to be a mad frog in your box.

Rob Shorney – If best buddies like you had to be purchased, I'd have to win the lottery, but maybe I already have.

David and Jami, Sheena and Ray, Hillary and Keith, Iain – First readers and friends of the first order. Your honesty, considered opinions, support and appreciation of my work humbles me.

My students from 2006–2015 from whom I observed and learnt so much about human development, behaviour and emotional response.

David Povilaitis – For your friendship, advice, support and book cover.

Everyone at Austin Macauley for all your hard work and believing what I write should be published and read.

Table of Contents

Keep away from people who belittle your ambitions. Small people always do that, but the really great make you feel that you, too, can become great.

Mark Twain

Introduction

I understand why self-help books are written and produced; indeed, I have read many. However, besides some notable exceptions, most have left me wondering if the writer has truly experienced walking in treacle or felt the overwhelming panic of being lost in a complicated maze of a height where the horizon cannot be seen. I've asked myself if they've tried to swim against the tide with no welcoming beach in sight or travelled for an eternity in a tunnel where there is nothing but the incessant lighting up of your smart phone, demanding it be answered; or if you do see a light in the distance, you discover it's a train coming towards you.

I'm not a fan of clichés and am usually reluctant to use them in prose or narrative; but I've let some off the leash to put the spotlight on how so many of us feel swamped with hopelessness, fear and self-doubt during certain times of our life.

I'm one of millions who have at some time questioned what we are doing and why; looking for guidance and directions as we meander through a soulless landscape trying to interpret the map of life. Wouldn't it be fun, and easier, if we could enter our desired life destination into a satellite navigation device, voiced over by our favourite actor or actress; who with soothing, calm tones, would make our journey stress free by avoiding traffic jams and other inconvenient hold ups or diversions, and advising when it would be a good time to pull off the road for rest and relaxation?

Unfortunately, the chances of that happening are more remote than a human landing on Pluto (I initially wrote Mars, but it's appearing more likely a lunatic will make it there one day ... I use the word lunatic because the chances of making it back would be slim, apparently).

Maybe our best chance of not only surviving, but enjoying life to a greater degree is to watch and learn from the wise individuals who have been there, done that, and bought the T-shirt; the tourist guides, who could recommend sights of interest to explore, places in which to eat, drink and be merry; but who also have the knowledge of areas we should stay away from so that we don't get mugged of our hard earned money and possessions: or even our lives if something or someone deceives us into believing that black is white or white is black.

Many of us would consider we have been content and confident most of our lives, but have learned, unfortunately, how certain situations can be instrumental in greasing any handle we thought we had on reality; these include: divorce, redundancy, death of close ones; I'm sure you could extend this list greatly by adding your own personal experiences.

This book has been wholly written from experiences I've gained from attending the University of Life. I've bumbled my way through, in part, by the common sense installed in me by watching and learning from my incredible parents.

I discovered motorcycling as the ultimate therapy for me by accident in 2001. From a twist of fate and changing circumstances, I decided to try something I'd always wanted to do but just hadn't the prior time due to other commitments. I took up motorcycling completely unaware of the positive changes it would make to my life; I embraced it from the start, enjoying the adrenaline rush and an excitement I hadn't experienced for some considerable time.

This is my retrospective look over the last 16 years that seem to have gone in a blink of the eye. My musings have been written with gentle humour and self-deprecation as I can now look back and smile at the mistakes I made; accepting I waded in copious amounts of self-induced stupidity, and wallowed in unnecessary self-pity because I ignored my own instinct – like many of us do – and succumbed to the emotional urge to help too many people too much of the time. I allowed myself to be constantly diverted from my planned path, leaving me increasingly disappointed and disillusioned: my authentic self was stranded and suffocating like a beached whale, cut off from the pod as a result of losing my bearings.

I found *my* bearings again from motorcycling. I re-built my confidence and self-esteem, and have learned to discriminate clearly between what is important to me and what is not. I have come to understand the difference between loneliness and solitude, and benefits from the latter. I make firmer – and speedier – decisions these days and accept disappointments more positively; I've also come to realise that the expression, 'procrastination is the thief of time' is so true.

Importantly, I have included a chapter where I debunk myths about motorcycling – a significant element of the book – in which I discuss many issues relating to the human condition that seem to rise up like impermeable and impenetrable barriers when we least expect them, or indeed want them … like a rattle snake in a lucky dip. It's been written to be read in a non-linear way, dipping into the sections that may have more relevance to your circumstance, but I do hope you read it all, if only to realise many of us experience the same issues that lead us, at some point, to ask the question; what is the meaning of life? I'm not sure the question has truly been answered, or ever will be.

Without sounding spiritual or self-indulgent, I have, through every single mile of the 250,000 I have ridden, learned so much about myself; so maybe the question should be; what is the meaning of *my* life? With confidence and self-belief we can become the air traffic controller responsible for the direction of our own destiny, and also the pilot guiding us safely through the clear skies -and turbulence – during the journey: and if the only thing you take from reading this book is that during the mayhem of the daily grind you never forget *yourself*, then I would see that as job done; and put a smile on my face in the process.

The fact is, we all seem to get carried away on the tide of expectation at work and at home, leaving what appears to be a tiny amount of time for play, rest and relaxation in our lives. Many people I have spoken to during the writing of this book have shown a wish and inclination to get off the bus, so to speak, but have been unable to summon up sufficient courage to push the bell, alerting the driver of their intention. I understand what it feels like, experiencing the frustration and confusion in your mind, balancing everything on the 'for and against' list when trying to make a decision. One of the main issues is that over time, we have somehow stopped relying on our own intuition, and developed a personal team of 'advisors', all of whom we refer to for an opinion – and some who offer an opinion when it's not actually been requested. I will cover these issues, and much more, not as absolute answers to problems, but more as guidance on how to clear the fog, to gain clarity and make better, well informed decisions; so as the air traffic controller, we can give clear, precise and explicit instructions to the pilot sitting in the cockpit of our minds.

Consumerism, technology and social media contribute greatly to the mix – and confusion – in modern society, leading us to believe that unless we get on board with it all, we will be left behind on the platform and become 'Billy no mates'. However, as most of us realise, having a million friends on face book, and thousands of 'likes' is about as far away from reality as you can get, and as soulless as a dead fish. Fortunately I've never had a problem with my own company, and riding a motorbike has reinforced the fact we all need time and space to think, appreciating the absence of any interruption, human or digital, that has an overbearing effect on us both physically and emotionally.

Working out what really matters in my life has taken far too many years, a great deal of heartache and a serious amount of soul searching; but one thing I do know and have learned from my journey, is that it is never too late to adjust the sails and start tacking to head in a more favourable direction.

This is a personal account from which you may pick up tips and hints – even short cuts – but I have been mindful not to suggest 'one must do this' or 'one must not do that' as it would be crass, and ignore the fact that we are all individuals, and have the freedom of choice to live our lives as we darned well please. I guess though, by reading this, you are looking for a deeper meaning, and have started the search as I did, for something, but not sure what, that will bring more calm and significance to your everyday existence. And in truth, this is what I have discovered through motorcycling; a way of discovering authenticity and a tranquillity that allows me to *live* everyday instead of *existing*.

I am sure there are many other activities that could produce the same result and in fact I had fun giving some of them a go. However, as will become clear in the following pages, motorcycling excited and engaged me from the start, and over the years has developed into a longstanding personal therapy; aside from the pure fun and adrenaline that still kicks in – 16 years on – every time I head off somewhere or anywhere on two wheels come rain or shine.

During my time as a motorcycle instructor I undertook plenty of training in the wet (well I do live in the UK) which perversely to some, I enjoyed, recalling that my dad often worked in downpours and he took the view that rain was simply liquid sunshine, which I thought was a great way of looking at it. There is a saying: 'Life is not about waiting for the storm to pass, it's about learning to dance in the rain', and has a resonance that my dad did, and I have, genuinely tried to live by.

With all that I have succeeded in, failed at, and learned over the last 16 years of riding, motorcycling has been instrumental in keeping me sane in an ever increasing insane world. I genuinely hope that you all find what you are looking for, and that the book will be of help in your search.

Chapter 1
The Beginning

This book, unknown to me at the time, was being written from the moment I first sat astride a motorcycle in the extreme cold of winter of 2000 – 2001 at a Birmingham training school. The excitement of starting to ride eclipsed any other thoughts in my mind. I did not feel the chill that would have frozen the testicles off a brass monkey and I cannot remember taking part in any Christmas festivities. I have no recall of bringing in the New Year – it had nothing to do with alcohol – because I was focussed on one thing and one thing only. I completed my compulsory basic training, (CBT), and went straight into my big bike training, (Direct Access). I passed my test on 31st January, 2001 on a cold crisp day with the sun making a cameo appearance.

I had a smile that went from ear to ear, high on adrenaline from initial training to obtaining my treasured category 'A' motorcycle licence. One of my intentions in writing this book is to encourage as many people to take up motorcycling for the benefits, and there are many which will be covered, and to experience the total freedom and spiritual feeling that any biker will only be too happy to explain. If you do ask, the first thing you will see is the grin that says it all.

The years have gone by in a flash, but I have always maintained the discipline to ensure my feet remain planted on the learning curve; through self-improvement, advanced training techniques and riding with talented, experienced riders. I have toured the United Kingdom and Europe, obtained my motorcycle instructor licence, set up and operated a training school, Spirit Rider, and achieved the highest civilian awards for motorcycling in the UK: Royal Society for the Prevention of Accidents (ROSPA gold) and The Institute of Advanced Motorcyclists (IAM first register). I was Chairman of West Midlands ROSPA advanced motorcycle training group for a short while during 2015.

During this time there have been painful, stressful, physical, and emotional situations to deal with, including; work, redundancy, marriage, divorce, house moves, and illness. I contracted Labyrinthitis in 2007, a debilitating viral infection of the hearing system affecting balance; this prevented me motorcycling, and playing guitar in my band for nine months: some wished it had stopped me singing. Rob, a great friend, and drummer in the band, has a theory that my marital issues (plural) all stemmed (note past tense) from my love of wedding cake … he may have a point.

2015 was a watershed year in my life. The death of my dad in February shook me to the core. He was my mentor and rock. We had always enjoyed a wonderful relationship which seemed to improve with age, just like a good wine. The space he has left in my life is impossible to describe. Every day there is an ache in my heart, but I have a photo of us together in the defunct road tax disc holder on my bike, and he rides with me wherever I go. Coincidentally, any remaining self-obsession I was guilty of disappeared with the passing of the most influential person in my life. It was a reminder that my beloved dad was someone who never saw whinging or complaining as productive or useful in his life, despite the incredible pain and suffering he endured during his final years.

The one consistent part of my life over this period has been motorcycling. Despite the difficult times I've encountered, I wanted to explore the possibility that motorcycling has been the best form of therapy for me over the last 16 years. Medication, meditation and counselling all popped up on the menu at various times, none of which had a significant or lasting effect. Riding my motorcycle though, has had a more beneficial and tangible affect in every aspect of my life. I taught around 2000 students from 2007 to 2015 and I have witnessed some incredible changes in their characters too; from the practical and physical side of handling a motorbike, to the effect bestowed on them at an emotional level in both their professional and private lives.

Chapter 2
Many Miles Later

I calculate I have travelled in excess of 250,000 miles since passing my test; a combination of commuting, training and touring. For me, motorcycling is exhilarating and totally absorbing, both physically and emotionally. Every piece of my body is used from head to toe and my brain is switched on like a high powered light bulb. It also engages the senses of sight, smell and hearing. The brain is never on idle whilst riding, but the really clever thing is it cuts the connection to any negative voices in your head; it treats them like a naughty child and ignores them until they calm down and start behaving again. The mind has other more pressing matters to deal with when riding: it requires your full attention.

And this is the point. I am completely engrossed in the technical part of riding; being in the correct gear; ensuring my bike is in the best position on the road, making adjustments when required; travelling at an appropriate speed for all weather, road and traffic conditions, the combination of which would test a chess grand master. I am continually assessing, scanning 360 degrees around me, and planning, looking as far as the sky line to look for and anticipate potential hazards which can either be fixed or moving. Your thoughts are concentrated on making progress; your mind does not have room to consider other information with no direct bearing on your riding or safety. In effect, you find yourself truly living in the moment.

Another intriguing aspect of motorcycling, because of the variables outlined above, is that two days are never the same. There can be obvious differences such as rain or sunshine, but there may be other more subtle changes like a small movement in temperature or strength of wind for example, all of which have to be taken into account when riding. Further, there will be physical effects on the bike that have to be considered such as tyre, brake pad and chain wear, plus running down from a full tank of fuel; all of which have a more discernible effect than in a car.

Now, after you've slipped on your leathers, helmet and gloves, your partner asks you to pick up some milk on your trip out. This will not, I assure you, be high on your list of priorities as you negotiate a sublime and complex series of bends, a multi entry and exit roundabout with numerous lanes that closer resembles a motorway, or if you simply stop for breakfast with your fellow bikers. You will feel so chilled and relaxed after your ride that any mental shopping list will have disappeared altogether. Facing consequences when you return home with no milk will not bother you one iota: it's not life threatening … usually.

I use this as an example because we've all had the experience where someone has asked us to do something, and enquires later whether we have done it. We admonish ourselves before the questioner does (their last word is usually 'idiot' preceded by a fruity expletive) trying to work out why you just couldn't remember that one task. The answer is simple; we're in the zone, in our own world where we submit ourselves to the fun factory in our mind that has actually been with us since childhood. For some, these times are few and far between and those they had have become a distant memory.

Chapter 3
Journey Of Life

Our train in life has numerous carriages, and stations it can stop at. As we progress to the next rung on the career ladder, buying a newer or larger house, replacing the car or increasing the population, we feel we are moving forward and making progress. The first carriage is our childhood, full of memories we picked up at our first few stops. Our intention, albeit well meaning, is to fill the other carriages with aspects of life and material goods we think will satisfy our needs and wants: so we start the venture with hope and enthusiasm.

The trouble is, at some point in our journey, we realise we've caught the express train that stops at very few stations and consequently makes it impossible to pick up anything useful. We could take stock of all the positive gains in our life, simply enjoy what we already have, and not consider putting anything more in the carriages. This sounds obvious but very few people stop to appreciate the enduring aspects of our lives; family, love and friendship for example.

Perhaps taking the stopper train would have been more appropriate, but boarded the one we assumed might get us to our destination quicker; only to find out on arrival it is only half full; and has been for most of the trip.

As we become older, gain wisdom and hopefully increase our yield of common sense, we search more for authenticity and spirituality in our lives to satisfy us and keep us contented during the journey, rather than wanting something regardless of whether we need it, and wanting it now, on the false premise it will make us feel good.

We do not consider it at the time, but we embark on a journey of self-perpetuating and ever decreasing circles, a quest for attainment that's usually unrealistic, and ends up as a fruitless search for the Holy Grail of happiness and pleasure. There is truth in the expression 'much wants more' and I often wonder how many people, consciously or not, are trapped in the web of conspicuous consumption, or to put it another way, 'keeping up with the Jones''. As free thinking adults we have to take some responsibility for this: but I also believe we are not entirely to blame.

Chapter 4
Choices

Situations in which we find ourselves are borne from expectations during our formative years; what we wanted to do and what we were expected to do were usually two different matters – especially as teenagers – and often question later in life how we find ourselves in the proverbial manure; a job we do not like; living in a house next door to the neighbours from hell; bringing up children who have an ability to morph into the devil at will, and further, treat your home like an hotel; owning a car that does everything but start in the winter; or living with someone who thinks changing you from the person you were when you first met is the necessary route to a happy relationship – I know, a little heavy that one, but you get the idea.

In fact, to digress a little if I may, my idea of marriage guidance would save a gargantuan amount of time, heartache and money by sticking warring couples into the same room, each armed with a pencil and paper, and suggest they write down what attracted them to each other in the first place, including details of their courting period before getting married. Only then would they be allowed to leave the room, if they agreed in writing, to begin the dating process again using their notes as a guide: I am convinced it would work and save many relationships from oblivion. However, Rob – my personal unpaid counsellor – would probably suggest, because of my penchant for confetti, that I stick to music, motorcycling and writing; to resist the temptation advising others on marital issues.

On a more serious note, it seems decision making is sometimes taken out of our hands, although it could be argued we are too often inclined to relinquish the responsibility. Making appropriate choices, or at least taking a path that would have suited us better, seems an art form reserved for the privileged few. The main problem of course is we don't walk around with a crystal ball or have a direct line to the oracle.

We may not remember the precise time in our lives that we started making choices, but we did, and we were very young when it started. As children we were subject to a great deal of corrective training – I tried to use a different word here, but couldn't find one that was more accurate – and generally it was both required and appropriate.

Being told what we could do and not do was often good for our health, aside from the fact it taught us by following some of the guidance, we worked out it prevented the big people from wagging fingers and reprimanding us. A typical example would have been learning not to place our fingers into what we now know is an electrical socket; an unhealthy activity, and even more dangerous if we had been licking our sticky fingers.

So, over the years we learned the difference between right and wrong, good and bad; just as importantly most of us were taught about truth, respect, civility and compassion. We lived our younger years according to this social engineering that we more usually call parenting, and the process was further perpetuated with the collusion of the teaching profession during our academic years. This is not a criticism per se, it's just the way I see it. From an early age we are raised with boundaries. Much as we need them to preserve our civilised life, I also feel that they can become shackles to a free mind, inventiveness, and individuality if we take them too far. They are like insurance policies, most of which are a necessary evil; humans are careless and have accidents or lose things, sometimes falling victim to those unpleasant individuals who prefer the five-fingered discount way of life.

Chapter 5
The Turning Point

It was during secondary education I had to make my first important decision. A decision that was mine and mine alone to make about subjects I would study to examination level; a decision that could potentially determine a direction in life. I'm not being melodramatic here. It worried me; I was 14 and considered mature for my age, but I did have self-doubt. Naturally, I took advice from my parents and teachers. However, it was both exciting and a little over whelming to be given the power to control a part of my future for the first time, taking responsibility for my own decisions and actions.

I did not have that feeling again until I sat on a motorbike and, under instruction, moved it forward twenty feet and came to a stop. Something tripped inside my head that day that set me free. I always thought song writing, and playing guitar in my band to a live audience – as opposed to a dead one, which some were – was a big deal, but this was not a bunch of young guys dreaming of fame and fortune, it was me, myself, I, at 40 years of age feeling at that moment, perhaps since childhood, that I hadn't got a care in the world.

But the cares and the troubles do come. Making further education or career choices; searching for the ideal partner; setting up home; starting a family, requiring inordinate communication, time and effort over a number of years.

However, this results in two things. Firstly, it is a leap on to the hamster wheel, and once aboard is difficult to get off as it never seems to stop; and have you noticed the wheel initially turns slowly, but without knowing exactly when, starts moving at the speed of a bullet, sending you into an uncontrollable spin? Secondly, as adulthood takes root, there is an inevitable drawdown on available leisure time and resources for those who previously engaged in multifarious ways of amusing themselves. Some even shut down completely and drop previously enjoyed activity as if it was forbidden fruit; a counter intuitive move in both the short and long term.

I understand, due to shifting priorities, money and time have to be assigned elsewhere. However, we seem to develop tunnel vision and a focus so targeted that we never look back on what we are leaving behind. This is a big mistake, primarily because we continue to conform to what society expects, instead of using our imagination and individuality to explore and investigate new ways of doing things.

We happily move forward, buying our first car, our first house, spending time and money on a wedding – usually to give a free jolly for relatives last spotted at your birth and who will only be seen again at a funeral; yours or theirs. Further, children come along and become part of the mix. Then guess what? As I suggested earlier we decide to start the whole process again; newer car, larger house and more children. The message seems to be, 'repeat process if still not fulfilled' or 'continue if you have a pathological draw to stress, tension, anxiety, resentment and chaos.'

You might be thinking that that's cynical and pessimistic. Not really. I refer back to social engineering and our propensity to follow what has gone before; it fits in with the way our parents were raised or indeed, the way they raised us. This can be a conscious decision we make, but I suspect most of us fall into line without fully realising the consequences that are, to be blunt, clearly signposted. We either believe it is the correct thing to do or something we must do. Rarely do we rely on our instincts and follow a path that dares to oppose our upbringing – and I am not talking about anarchy here – but where we find the key to the door that releases our uniqueness as individuals. Many people are extremely happy following a prescription for life, and I am not here to denigrate it. Far from it; like my parents, many people find ultimate joy and meaning in life, by creating life.

What I am suggesting, is that we need to build sufficient self-confidence to break out of our comfort zones if we consider our life has hit the buffers. It may even be that our train didn't leave the station first time round. Many individuals fall at the first hurdle by making benign statements such as:

'It's the way it's always been.'

'I'm not in a position to change.'

'I made my bed so I'll have to lie in it.'

All misguided of course, but in the midst of turmoil, wondering how you signed up to become a juggler, one thing becomes apparent; your hands are not on the steering wheel attached to the vehicle of life.

We may not even be in the vehicle of our choosing. I had always wanted to become a writer or musician but my aspirations and dreams went south after I left school. In the final year of education, which included careers advice, I was left in no doubt that these were only 'hobbies' and I should, instead, think about a steady career in the civil service, banking, accounting, engineering or retail. I don't think the irony has been lost on many; taking advice from a careers master whose only job was, well, to give career advice. I did consider newspaper Journalism as a way of writing, and investigated the possibilities; but after spending a week at a large regional paper, I quickly came to the conclusion that Journalism is the magpie profession in terms of writing, and I wanted to be more authentic and original with my subject matter.

However, I was the first boy in my secondary school to join a short-hand and typewriting class, which raised eyebrows and sniggers from fellow pupils: I can only assume everyone thought it was just a jolly jape to be in a class full of girls. Three of my mates though were the first boys in school to join cookery classes, so I was in good company. Back in the mid to late 1970's, all this was unusual (and previously unthinkable); cookery and shorthand were considered courses for girls, and metal or wood work were boys only classes. I like to think my school friends and I were trendsetters; these days it is a free for all with no silly barriers in place to prevent anyone studying what they wish: how times have changed.

Quite what happened next is a mystery, although I have to admit the chance of earning serious money for the first time skewed my thoughts in terms of wants and needs. I did take a job in the civil service. I appreciate looking back it was my leap onto the hamster wheel that turned many times for too many years before I gained the confidence to jump off; exhausted and mentally drained.

Referring back to my analogy, I travelled on that train for the journey, with other passengers heading in the same direction, before I found the courage to disembark and ride solo on a motorbike – metaphorically speaking, as it was some years before I sat on one. Since then my life has been very similar to motorcycling. I have chosen the route and picked the stopping off points. I also choose the speed I travel, always adjusting it to the prevailing circumstances.

There are times when I ride quickly when it is safe to do so; there are times when I slow everything down and take everything in, appreciating the view.

I also re-discovered solitude, something so significant and precious, yet I wondered how it was possible I had mislaid it – a bit like my virginity. As a result I also re-engaged with silence, the value of which I had underestimated; it gave me the space to reflect without any digital or human interruption, and I have been able to make firmer decisions, and say 'no' more often without fear of upsetting anyone. The most significant lesson I learned was there is nothing wrong enjoying your own company, or your own personal environment. *Your* space, *your* time, and *your* thoughts, are often invaded by *too many* people with *too many* opinions, and *too much* technology with *too much* control over your life. It is that simple. There will be further references to these thoughts later.

Sitting on that train in a trance, life outside flashing by, I decided I wanted to be part of the adventure film that was taking place on the other side of the window. We are all capable of making significant and positive change in our lives. We can either find the brake to the hamster wheel or summon sufficient courage to do as I did, eventually, and take a leap into the unknown. I used to discuss many of my ideas and plans with my dad, and he used to say, 'If something has been done by someone, then it can theoretically be done by anyone, including you!' His logic is hard to fault. I suspect my dad always knew I believed in that, and after many years, in myself too. It was his way of saying, 'go for it son.'

Chapter 6
Discover For Yourself

I'd always wanted to ride motorbikes, but for my most of my working life I'd had careers involving a great deal of travel in the UK and abroad. Secondly, my main interest was music during this period and I spent most of my leisure time either rehearsing or gigging.

However, it didn't stop opinions being offered on why I shouldn't take up riding a motorbike; but is it not often the case if you question someone's motive for doing something it simply feeds their desire to carry on regardless. It wasn't my motive; I have always been insatiably inquisitive: I just had to find out for myself. So I think this is a good place to debunk the myths peddled by individuals who have no interest in the sport and, furthermore, have acquired a hero worship syndrome for their own voice: you know who I'm talking about.

If you do have thoughts about trying something new (it could be adventurous or not) the key is to keep them to yourself until you have researched any subject matter; arm yourselves with facts and figures as it will be easier to counter any objection from those individuals who always seem to have a negative opinion about so much. Even better – and this is my preferred option – kick off your new ambition without telling a soul, the shock factor alone is worth watching and is usually an odd mixture of disbelief and admiration. Should anyone close to you react negatively, then I would guess a deeper problem exists that needs attention: it may ultimately lead to someone reaching for their coat, but if respect is not being given or reciprocated, then a hard decision is often best for the sake of sanity; and is something I wished I had learned sooner.

Chapter 7
The Myths

- Motorbikes are dangerous
- I can't afford it
- It's a midlife crisis
- I don't have the time
- I don't have the aptitude
- I'm too old
- It's not for women

Motorbikes Are Dangerous

For those who are astute and have a love of the English language, you will note the above statement does not make sense. How can a motorbike be dangerous? Many who do not ride a motorbike will throw that statement at you, yet it has no meaning. What they are attempting to say? For this sentence to begin to make grammatical sense you'd have to substitute the word motorbike (noun) for motorcycling (verb). If people want to be pedantic with me about what I should or shouldn't do with my own time, then I'm going to be pedantic about them using the English language correctly; keep reading and all will be revealed.

Prior to 1990, some training schemes were available in the UK, but the accident rate was admittedly quite shocking. The current compulsory basic training process was introduced in 1990, and since then the accident rate has reduced year on year. 2009 saw the introduction of a comprehensive off road test prior to the on road examination, required for any motorcycles to be ridden on the road without learner plates. This has resulted in motorcyclists riding on the public road in the UK with a greater skill set than at any time since testing was introduced in 1935.

However, many activities have associated risks, even walking down the street. There are numerous things in life that are potentially dangerous, a large number of them can be found in the home: a boiling kettle, a sharp set of kitchen knives; power tools, and so on. It's possible to purchase a chainsaw from your local hardware store, receive no training on how to use it, and leave the store without buying any protective equipment. A fellow motorcycle instructor I worked with, a former Royal Air Force weapons trainer, suggested a loaded gun on a table is not dangerous, which is true; just like a car with the engine turned off and the handbrake on.

So what have all the above in common? They are inanimate objects, and by definition cannot be dangerous. However, all the above can become potentially lethal when we introduce the human element. Yes, the bad news is we are to blame for turning these dormant pieces of equipment into killing machines. The point is, there is risk associated with everything we do, the list is endless, but the common denominator that increases risk to the point of injury or death is you and me. Machinery is harmless until we get our hands on it. There will be a warning notice attached to the chain saw; unfortunately there won't be one attached to the novice tree feller.

Motorcycle training is a legal requirement in most countries around the world. In Europe there is a common training process overseen by government transport departments. Similar training programs are in place across the globe. These initial schemes usually take place in safe off road areas. When a satisfactory level of competence is achieved through a combination of class room and training ground work, tuition is continued on the public highway.

So, there we are. We have discovered that 'motorbikes' are not dangerous, humans are, but minimising the risk of potential dangers by undertaking thorough and professional training is the key to safe and effective riding; in fact you might say it is the key to safe and effective anything.

I Can't Afford It

This one is easy to deal with. The first thing to do here is add up the total amount your car costs per annum to keep it on the road. You'll be shocked at the figure. Don't forget to include road tax, insurance, mot test (annual vehicle condition assessment in the UK), fuel, spares, repairs, tyres, car parking charges, and any fines for motoring offences you may have accrued (regardless of whether you feel they were justified or not).

Now, let's take a look at the costs involved in owning a motorcycle. Insurance is generally lower because unless you are using your motorcycle for commuting, the miles covered and the time you are on the public highway is less than a car; your age, experience, engine size of your bike and area where you live will be taken into account.

UK motorcycle road tax is split into four bands depending on the engine size of the bike. An interesting point arises here; if motorcycle road tax was based on emissions as it is for cars, then all motorcycles would be subject to lower road tax than current rates. For example, cars between 700cc and 1.2cc pay between £20 and £30 per annum, whereas motorcycle road tax for the same cc level is currently £86. Emissions are not part of the UK MOT test for motorcycles which, without being cynical, may suggest the authorities would feel uncomfortable with the results if they *were* tested. You can draw your own conclusions from this about the intent of government to promote motorcycles as a greener alternative to cars; they also take up less space and cause far less damage to roads: it does, however, raise a substantial amount of cash for the treasury.

As I write, there has been a significant drop in world oil prices, although cartels have agreed to reduce production, so increased prices at the pump will be imminent. Whilst operating my training school, Spirit Rider, the cost of petrol peaked at gonad kicking and eye watering rates. Today it is available for a more reasonable cost per litre. Modern motorcycles are also highly efficient, and most 125cc commuter machines should return a minimum of 100 miles to the gallon.

City centre car parking charges are high, and are unlikely to decrease like petrol. But that's fine, because I have never seen charges for parking motorcycles anywhere in the UK or abroad, and motorcycle parking is usually in, or very close to, town or city centres.

Training costs have not risen with inflation, and I write from experience. Most schools I'm in contact with continue to work on pricing from five years ago or more. Initial training will allow you to ride a 125cc machine solo – with learner plates – until you decide to train and pass your test on a larger machine.

Always visit the training school when booking so you can assess the standard and cleanliness of the premises, bikes and protective equipment. If possible, meet the instructor who will be taking your training. This is often overlooked, but you will be with them for some time, and you really do need to know it is someone you will be comfortable with. The majority of instructors are experienced trainers with a great sense of humour and have patience that knows no bounds; most would also make great politicians and psychotherapists so you'll be in good hands. If you do unfortunately find one that bites, report it to the authorities; it has obviously slipped its leash and as a licensed animal will be returned to its owner for remedial training.

A safety helmet is a legal requirement, and protective clothing is essential. It has to fit your head perfectly so I would always visit a local dealer to try it before you buy. Small, medium and large mean very little to motorcyclists who take their safety seriously. Retailers in the motorcycle industry are invariably bikers, they understand the helmet is a priority piece of kit and will spend as much time with you as it takes to ensure you have the correct fit. Legal and appropriately tested helmets for the UK market extend through a wide cost range. Because of its design a helmet is a one impact device – and this includes accidentally dropping it from a height of three feet or more – so always buy what you can afford to replace.

Pricing for clothing is competitive due to the plethora of high street and internet suppliers, and a search on eBay could save you even more money. Jacket, trousers, gloves and boots are essential for obvious reasons as we do not have the outer metal shell protecting us. But as we continue our journey through this book, we will discover the adrenalin surge and an emotional, even spiritual freedom, that comes from being on the outside of our mode of transport and not imprisoned by it.

I am not suggesting for a moment you swap your Chelsea tractor for the latest high tech whizz bang motorcycle, as problems will arise; your children will complain about having to use their legs for the school run

– or should that be walk; the wife may not be too pleased if you suggest catching a bus to get your weekly shop; and the in-laws will take a dim view of suggesting they call a cab to come over for Sunday lunch. However, to recreate the lost sense of adventure and as an answer to the issues above, you could buy spare safety helmets and a full pannier kit: sorted.

As for most hobbies and pastimes, motorcycling requires an initial outlay but we have to keep a sense of perspective on costs. I have been involved in music since school days and over the years I have spent inordinate amounts of money on guitars, associated equipment and travelling.

Prior to getting on a motorcycle I was involved in serious jet-skiing with a bunch of guys who made it an extreme sport – bum squeaking extreme. Fuel consumption was unbelievable. None of us had an oil sheik as an uncle so we reluctantly decided after four years to hang up our lanyards (lanyard; a safety key requirement for waterborne craft should you make an unscheduled dismount).

My elder brother, and younger sister have been racing cyclists, and I point out to them they have spent thousands of pounds on bikes that don't even have an engine. Yes, I have spent money on motorcycling, but the rewards have justified every penny spent. I own and still wear a quality Italian leather motorcycling jacket I bought 17 years ago, but due to an increasing waistline, I cannot admit to owning my original leather trousers which were part of a two piece suit: but you can't have it all.

I have covered this from the monetary aspect of "I can't afford it." Towards the end of this book, I want you to consider the same statement from a spiritual and emotional point of view, and I hope there will be many of you saying, "I can't afford not to."

It's A Mid-Life Crisis

I came to motorcycling later in life at the age of 40, and I will say from the outset, my decision to ride motorbikes had nothing to do with a midlife crisis. In my view the term is nonsense. Put simply, life is a fluid process based on changing circumstances. Living life is the act of moving from one situation to another, dealing with changes as they occur: it is how we deal with these shifting sands that can either result in leading a happy contented life, or one that can lead the brain into a permanently bewildered state.

I am writing this from a personal perspective, and as I have experienced, the alternative to positive action could lead to extreme physical and mental exhaustion. I would urge anyone to seek professional help or guidance in the first instance if you find yourself floundering; there are some wonderful organisations and people out there that can help.

The word *crisis* is inappropriate. An alternative word might be *change*; a better word is *opportunity*. It may be you resign from your job, either through careful consideration or from a fit of pique. It makes no difference; you'll have no career either way. What you certainly will do is open doors leading to possibilities you could only dream of. Informing HR your job belongs where the sun doesn't shine will be a bonus; childish, but deliciously satisfying.

The kids have left home. Some people will say 'so what' others will be saying 'now what?' The 'now what?' brigade are a split bunch, divided between the rhetorical theorists – who know exactly what they're going to do and when – or those genuinely asking how they will fill their time before the first visit to son or daughter's university … and can't work out immediately why their offspring chose to study so far away. After new barrels have been fitted to locks and the moat has been restocked with piranha, three things become apparent once kids have flown the coup.

Firstly: you will have available income. This is initially a little confusing; you will think a utility bill has remained unpaid, or you have left the supermarket without paying for groceries.

Secondly: keeping with the food theme, you will notice visits to the aforementioned supermarket are less frequent. Remarkably, this is because food seems to stay in your fridge longer, leading you to think the mice have packed their bags and gone with the kids. If you feel new locks for the front door is extreme you could put a lock on the fridge to preserve stocks during visiting hours; dad often joked that my siblings and I only visited to put our noses in mum's snack cupboard or fridge, and of course she only filled them because we were coming.

Thirdly: time; this without doubt is the most important factor and valuable commodity with no exception. Again, this can be confusing in the early days of your new found freedom if only because your duty as a taxi-driver has finished. You'll be at home wondering if you should be picking the kids up from school, or thinking you have left them somewhere but can't remember where. No more evening clubs or sports events at weekends either. It will leave you wondering why waking up with the larks is necessary, but this situation does resolve itself, and quite quickly if you allow it and start doing things for yourself again.

From here on in, I would like you to relegate 'mid-life crisis' to room 101 and only think about mid-life opportunity; take stock of where you are in your life, realise that time waits for no one, and utilise your rediscovered income and time as if you were born again. You might get enjoyment from enrolling on a pottery or poetry course, taking up knitting or jam making, or decide that jumping out of an aeroplane with a back pack stuffed with a large handkerchief – hoping it will open as you have been promised – is something that will excite you and reinvigorate your zest for life. Motorcycling will offer you as much if not more – and you have come this far, so let's read on.

A final point that may convince you if you haven't already worked it out; most crises occur when the kids are at home; in relation to growing up, adolescence, education and health. Issues may well transpire later on, but remember they are adults after the age of 18 and any emotional or financial input will be a choice you voluntarily make and not from any legal obligation. I am not suggesting cutting them loose and leaving them to their own devices entirely, but the dynamic has changed. Helping is one thing but interfering may encroach on their initiative and new found independence; consider how you felt at their age. Remember, this is your chance to take up new challenges, to be adventurous or creative; to be you again.

I Don't Have The Time

I have discussed time that is created once the children have left home, but it is time available many people think they do not have before this point we need to examine.

Bed companies entice us into buying their products by informing us we spend about a third of our lives sleeping; a unique selling point not missed by many. We can point to medical surveys suggesting we benefit from at least six hours of sleep to reduce the chances of developing depression, stress, diabetes and obesity to name a few; it also ensures our brains will perform at the highest level. Is it not strange then, that many people believe time sleeping is time wasted despite research showing the opposite is true? I'm a committed believer in the adage 'sleep is a cure for many ills' and I'm brazenly at ease with my personal sleep budget which, if presented as a pie chart, would clearly show the close relationship and love I have for my duvet.

So, this means we are awake for two thirds of our lives, which seems sufficient time to undertake effective tasks and productive activities if we choose to. The problem; *life* is in the way; or is it? As mentioned previously, resources, particularly time, are so stretched that Jesus making five fish and two loaves a meal for thousands, seem as easy and effortless as a David Beckham goal scoring free kick; whereas most of us could use the services of a magician to extricate the maximum from our available free time. However, all is not lost.

Firstly, the arithmetic; we are given 24 hours in one day. That equates to eighty-six thousand, four hundred seconds to spend, and our aim should be to use every single one of them: remember, we cannot carry them forward so if you don't use them, you'll lose them, it's that straight forward.

Next, we have to carry out an unscientific, broad analysis of how we spend our time when we're not sleeping. I have to generalise here because detailing how all families live would take as long as it took Samuel Johnson to compile the English dictionary (nine years) and I suspect we'd all lose the will to live during the process.

To paraphrase from a Morecombe and Wise TV comedy sketch, these maybe the right words but not necessarily in the right order: shower, breakfast, brush teeth, dress oneself, dress little ones followed by the school drop, commute to work, eight hours labour, return commute, shower, evening meal, washing up. If you have a supportive extended family, the children are at home before you arrive, and may well have been fed and watered too. After a shower or soak in the bath we adorn casual wear for the evening ahead.

Let's assume at this point the kids have been entertained, homework completed. We may now be looking at the big hand on twelve and the small hand on eight; I appreciate some of you might think 'I wish.' However, it's what people do next that I want to highlight and I hope you will dig deep to find the ruthless honesty within yourselves that will make sense of the following thoughts.

Award yourself a treat if you: sit and relax with a book – you could either stroke it or read it; listen to music; converse with your loved ones; take an evening stroll, with or without a dog; jog or go to the local pool for a swim? In essence do you relax before going to bed, experiencing a tranquillity that is impossible to experience during the day, and slowing the brain down so it's prepared for a healthy six to eight hours of sleep; which in turn will repair the mind and body to take on the following day with vigour, enthusiasm and perhaps a little humour?

Or, do you switch on the television to watch your favourite program only to find you are still watching 'other stuff' up to the minute you go to bed? How many of you check emails, face book, tweet, or send texts throughout the entire evening, ignoring those closest around you? How many of you do all this in bed?

I'm no Luddite, far from it. The digital age has in many respects made life easier, and I appreciate being able to bank and shop on line when it suits me. And alas, through using zillions of digital noughts and ones, we use far less paper than ever before, and as a consequence have saved millions of trees across the planet; 'paperless' becoming the de facto approach to document storage.

I use technology a great deal, but I have always made one thing clear: technology will never control me. I value my personal time, particularly with my other half, so I have adopted a ruthless digital unplugging process, something I put into place after returning from a 'rebalancing' holiday I took in 2013; which I'd like to refer to – if only to remind me of what the sun looks like.

I set up my training school in a recession, a year after the financial melt-down in 2008, calculating that people would turn to a more economical – and more convenient – mode of transport. Although this turned out to be the case, what I hadn't, and couldn't have anticipated, were the two subsequent dire winters of 2009/2010 and 2010/2011, during which I lost twelve and eight weeks of teaching respectively due to snow; followed by the long months of torrential rain during spring and summer of 2011 which scuppered another four weeks of business. This resulted in working 12 to 14 hours a day, seven days a week for a considerable duration to make up for lost time and income (the joys of self-employment).

By January of 2012 I was feeling jaded and decided to seek out some winter sunshine in the Canary Island of Fuerteventura, to relax in some warmth and decide how I was going to organise my business for the New Year. So I could repose during my first break for four years I did the following: firstly, I switched my mobile phone on for a maximum of thirty minutes each day to call family and deal with business matters. Secondly, I removed my watch, so I could drop into a natural rhythm and take my head completely away from being 'mindful' of the time. I suffered no withdrawal symptoms. In fact, I experienced a tangible relief because I was not glancing at my watch or smart phone every few seconds, the digital twitch as I call it … note the word twit with a c and h added. Thirdly, I made no attempt to collect emails, the ruination of a holiday in my opinion – and perhaps the quickest route to divorce or parting of the ways should you do this with your wife or partner observing (interesting to note corporate businesses starting to disconnect employee's work email accounts whilst taking annual leave – absolutely right).

Long periods of abstinence from alcohol whilst teaching and riding are normal, so lying in the sun with a beer and Jack Daniels chaser contributed to the speed a hedonistic mood enveloped me; and the urge to make some early notes for this book … if alcohol only increased the rapidity of my writing each day to the same pace.

Whilst my phone is now on for most of a day, I restrict its use, and often switch it off around 8pm. I also believe there is no harm in asking people to refrain from calling you after a certain hour, because there is only so long one can put up with a barking dog (literally and metaphorically in my case, because I changed my ring tone to a barking dog; many find it amusing and see the irony, others, without a sense of humour, look on with disdain … well, disdain on I say). Finally, I stopped watching television; it was simply stealing too much time and found myself getting caught up watching mind numbing bilge for most of an evening, interspersed with advertisers effectively telling me my life would be poorer if I didn't purchase their product – bed manufacturers excepted of course.

I write at various times of the day so my lap top is usually on. However, I am pleased about the discipline I have developed in terms of its use and again this has been easier than I had anticipated. I use the internet for research whilst writing, and use it for emails, shopping or banking when I'm not. Sounds easy now, but it did require having a chat with oneself regularly in the early stages of this self-flagellating therapy.

Paradoxically, although world- wide communication has moved into a positive new era in many respects, our closer friend and family connections have been rapidly reduced to digital contact via text, face book, tweeting and other social media, losing the human value of face to face discussion that has seen a comparative rise in discourtesy, an increase in bad manners and a grotesque rise in disregard for safety, particularly whilst driving (maybe it should be called anti-social media). But this is the point; by controlling the digital interruption in my life, and removing the television factor, I have found many hours to spend more fruitfully. This has meant regaining regular face to face involvement with my family and friends, increased solitude, silence and space to think or reflect and put many issues into perspective, most of which had given me unnecessary fear and concern. On a practical level I now complete more tasks than I undertook previously and importantly, at a less frenetic pace.

Although I am busy writing, I have, because of my self-imposed and partial digital detoxification, found time for playing guitar and song writing again. I retained my motorcycle training licence though I no longer teach for a living, but have gained sufficient hours to train '*the boss*', and the pleasure of seeing someone achieve a dream is, and always has been the most rewarding result from instructing; apart from the fact I now have my favourite person as a riding partner.

I am not suggesting a radical change of lifestyle is the answer, but here's the thing; I regained three hours a day to use in other ways since I stopped watching television. That alone amounts to twenty-one hours a week. The second calculation has been easy to work out in terms of internet and smart phone use. I have not used social media for a while, and I have restricted the time I surf the net for services or products. My texts are short, monosyllabic, and consist of 'yes' or 'no', with the occasional 'maybe' thrown in and I have instructed I be shot if I start tweeting useless information or pictures of my dog's dinner. This process has gained about another hour a day, making a saving of twenty-eight in total.

I can't think of anything more useful than gaining over one complete day every week to do with what I will. This amounts to just short of five days a month, gaining sixty-one days over a year. This equates to around nine weeks, which is more annual leave entitlement than most people receive. To put it another way, it would mean watching television for one year in every six – that is rounding the figures up. The figure is shocking, and I suspect if I audited my past TV viewing more closely, the ratio would be closer to one year in every five.

'I don't have the time' does now seem to have lost its power to convince. The choice is yours how you spend your time, but with a little discipline and recalibration of where you want to be in life, anything is possible. We can find the hours required; we just have to find the will to effect change that could give us a more fulfilled existence.

I Don't Have The Aptitude

Where do our negative thoughts originate because, as far as I am aware, we're not born with them? I suspect the bad press that sometimes surrounds motorcycling is partly to blame. People who would love to give it a go are discouraged by the inane statement we started off with that 'motorbikes are dangerous,' or question 'Why do you want to do that?' or dictate 'I won't allow you to do that!' The significant thing to remember is all who have muttered those silly words have never been near a motorbike and have knowledge of motorcycling that would fit on the leg of a gnat.

There are too many people on this planet who are willing to give an unsolicited, and usually uninformed, opinion; irritating, if it's clear they have no knowledge of the subject they are talking about. Arm chair critics are pervasive and should be avoided where possible should you not wish to die of boredom, or if their views destroy or diminish your confidence. Keeping with the gnat theme, these opinions and negative statements can bite and leave a mark that will take time to heal, especially if we are of a sensitive nature; and whether we admit it or not, most of us are. Gnats are usually found near streams and rivers, so here's a suggestion; stay away from the water.

The dictionary definition of aptitude states it is 'a natural ability to do something,' and I suspect defining aptitude even gave our old friend Samuel Johnson some sleepless nights. I outlined above we are not born with negative thoughts, and I think it is also important to note we do not come straight from the womb playing virtuoso violin either; and contrary to what some car drivers think when using hand signals absent in the Highway Code, they were not delivered by the midwife and immediately placed behind a steering wheel.

We were all born ignorant and helpless, which means physically and emotionally at least, we all started on a level playing field. I haven't mentioned any financial advantages, because as babies we have no comprehension of, well, anything. We are equal. Given appropriate support and encouragement through our formative years, along with focus and hard work, we should realise anything is possible: achievement though, will never come unless you begin the process, but continue reading and you will understand how easy this can be once fears are allayed.

Dr Johnson's definition of ability is 'the possession of the means or skill to do something.' It may seem from my comments above that we don't appear to be born with anything much; but we are, and it's one of the greatest assets that most of us are not aware of in our early years, and completely misunderstand or take for granted in our later years.

The first miracle is that we are born. The second miracle is we are endowed with the innate ability to learn without lifting a single one of our tiny infant digits. This in time enables us to develop skills and attributes which we can use in many areas of our lives. So my question is this; at what time in our lives do we decide that something is not possible or achievable? Think about this for a few seconds. Strange, isn't it, when you ask yourself the same? Don't worry if the answer doesn't immediately pop into your head as I don't want you thinking too much about the past; what you do today and what you have planned for tomorrow are the important issues.

I am willing to bet my shirt – not a great prize admittedly, as I only ever wear a white t-shirt and blue jeans; I just hope the sweat is worth something – you have already compiled a mental list of people who have influenced your actions through negative words or statements; wondering how it is they held sufficient power over you preventing you from doing something that could have made your life more enjoyable, if not necessarily easier.

Despite what any teacher, parent, partner, or employer may have said – the list is unfortunately a long one – it is critical you remember one thing; this life remains yours from start to finish; your mind is *your* mind. They don't belong to anyone else, and I include any form of deity in this. Absolutely no one has any right over them, not physically, not emotionally: fact. If you ever have doubt about what you are doing, or should anyone oppose you, re-read this paragraph to yourself, or even better, write it down where you can't help but see it every day.

I appreciate manipulative and pernicious individuals exist amongst us, but you have to remember they are immature and insecure bullies who need professional help and guidance, and as some of you will know, there are people who make the list that would raise the most stubborn of eyebrows; and here I include people with power in the work place, home, religion and politics.

As I discovered during my time in business you need to be particularly vigilant; there is a fine line between power and abuse and some individuals often confuse the two, demanding reverence when in fact they are entitled to nothing of the sort. I have seen confidence and initiative crushed in the work place and this has often affected an individual's home and personal life too. I taught a number of students whose lack of self-esteem and confidence started at work, and one of the benefits of taking up motorcycling has gone some way to rebuilding their self-belief and to regain a feeling of control over their own lives; more on this in the chapter dedicated to the benefits of motorcycling. For now, the only power you need to consider developing is the one that will give you the mental strength to become *empowered*.

I have covered a number of issues preventing you from starting something new, but the key is to understand you are not alone, and millions of other people are also unsure about taking first steps to change. At Spirit Rider I often heard students say 'I can't' when attempting certain procedures. I would respond 'Well that's fine, but you do know there is no 'T' in can.' In order to learn, and increase our ability in something, to discover whether we have an aptitude for it, we need to change our attitude to learning.

One of the strangest things I hear is 'I couldn't do that because I know nothing about it,' the fear element of getting on a motorcycle absent in the statement; the fear being they have no knowledge of the 'subject', a perverse view, mentally putting a block in the way even before attempting a new skill. The trick is simple. We need to change our negative thoughts to positive ones, and follow this through with positive words and affirmations. Look in the mirror when you do this; vanity, I promise you, will not be a thought in your mind. It may seem childish to begin with, but children don't have problems trying anything new; in fact they relish and thrive in the learning process. For a long time, I have firmly believed that childhood should be for life, and not just for children; and remember, we need play time just as much as they do.

Now, I'm going to let you into a secret; and then I want you to be my disciples and tell your family and friends; I promise no harm will come to you; in fact it might release the shackles within you, self -imposed or forced on you through brain washing or negative and repetitive criticism.

The main barrier with starting to study, or learn a new skill, is down to one word; *FAILURE*. It haunts us from the second we have a thought we might like to try something different. The neon sign flashes continuously with all the criticisms and negative statements we have been forced to endure: 'Are you sure about this?' 'You really shouldn't.' 'You can't!' 'You, that's laughable.' 'What are you thinking?' 'What if something happens?' The last question is interesting, and could be answered with 'you mean what happens if I like it?'

I'm not literally suggesting criminal damage, but what would happen if we took a hammer to the neon sign? I could suggest we simply unplug it; but it would be too easy to plug it back in; piecing the neon sign back together would be a little more problematical.

To put all this into perspective we have to look at achievement more closely, and to do this we need an example to examine. As I'm writing, the Great Britain Olympic team has just returned from the 2016 games in Rio, Brazil. Unless you were hibernating, you will know the team finished second in the medals table, ahead of China and behind America. But the point has been made, if you consider the size of the UK and the USA, each of our gold medals was gained by a smaller percentage of the population.

This success was no accident. Investment in training programs was examined post-Olympic games of Atlanta in 1996 after achieving one gold medal. Subsequent investment has grown exponentially, particularly through sponsorship and lottery funding, and our haul of medals has grown in every tournament since. The point is that none of the athletes were born pole vaulting, sailing, cycling, or running 100 metres in less than ten seconds. They have all gone through a lengthy training process with coaches to reach a competitive level. There would have been failures along the way, but many people in sport, and indeed, business, have declared how their failures have played an important part in eventual success: Abraham Lincoln talked of failure being a constituent element in the achievement process.

So, there is the secret; we need failure. Failure is good if we learn lessons from it. Failure is a concept to be welcomed and not feared, because if we don't conquer fears we remain victims to them. My view is that the person who has never made a mistake hasn't been born yet, and is unlikely to be. For those arrogant enough to say they have never failed, Abraham Lincoln would have probably retorted 'then you've learned nothing.'

We are all born with the ability to learn, and if you take a moment to consider what you have learned and achieved since birth, doesn't it now feel a little lame not to consider learning a new skill? Let's put negativity from outside sources aside for a moment; the only person who truly stops you trying anything new … is yourself.

I'm Too Old

From a legal perspective much has changed over recent years in terms of equality. It's still not perfect, but there is less prejudice in the work place for example than previously experienced. However, it is personal views I find interesting when it comes to age and gender, hence this section and the next one which talks about women in motorcycling. I'm proud to say on a general level, motorcycle training has never experienced prejudice of any kind, because all government authorised training schools would immediately dismiss an instructor if unsavoury views were articulated through words or actions. Motorcycling is for everyone, and I develop this theme later in the book when I discuss the motorcycling fraternity.

In the UK, 16 is the age at which you can take motorised two wheels on to the public highway, albeit on a 50cc moped, until the age of 17 when this can be increased to a 125cc machine. This is graduated up to the age of 24 when you can train to ride larger machines. There is no upper age limit, but there may be other restrictions placed on your licence which normally relate to health issues. If you are physically and mentally able, riding well into your twilight years is possible; the benefits of keeping physically and mentally alert, enjoying the company of others, are obvious.

The oldest student I trained at Spirit Rider was 66, and there were others in their early 60's. This number increased for the over 50's; the majority of trainees were between 30 and 45, closely followed by the 24 to 29 age group. In terms of confidence, there were some interesting differences across the age range. Those from 16 to 24 were highly confident with a lower degree of safety and awareness; 25 to 45 year olds were confident, but this often developed into a variance of overconfidence, particularly in terms of making progress at the expense of safety and awareness. The over 45's lacked initial confidence which impacted on their early training. They showed exceptional awareness but this did not always transfer into efficient progress, keeping up with traffic on higher speed limits for example, for which there are perfectly valid safety reasons to do so.

It became easy to identify those that could have benefited from further enhanced training after having passed their test; however, all showed sufficient competency to ensure they could ride solo on the public highway without being a danger to themselves or the public.

There are many publications – suggesting new things to do – aimed at people who have taken retirement – early or otherwise and for many reasons – and my suggestion would be to purchase one, or more, as your new challenge bible; I believe passionately it's never too late to learn new skills, particularly if they are fun related; but do remember to check with your doctor if the intended activity is strenuous, or has the potential to increase your heart rate to previously uncharted levels. If white water rafting appeals to you, remember that learning to swim does take priority:

there are no such pre-requisites for learning to ride a motorcycle: except for common sense of course.

It's Not For Women

This is not a platform for jokes from men about women taking up a 'male' activity. The buffoons who have an old boys' school way of looking at life have no right to make comment or decide that certain activities, or organisations, should or shouldn't be open to women. It is preposterous, for example, it took until recent times for women to be ordained as priests; and to women golfers who remain excluded from exclusive clubs around the UK and the world, I say 'hang up your irons, retire your personalised balls, or insert them where you've wanted to put them for years – but do remember men have a lower pain threshold – and join one of the largest and friendliest communities in the world.'

The motorcycling fraternity welcomes women; I cannot put it in simpler or fewer words. Ladies, you will be treated the same as gentlemen from the moment you contact a training school to enquire about lessons and to passing your test and beyond. Should you suspect for a micro second that you are not being taken seriously, it is most likely you have contacted a rare specimen last seen walking the earth with dinosaurs; do not hand over your pink pound, it will be valued and respected elsewhere. Interestingly, the number of women taking up motorcycling – in the UK – is currently growing at twice the rate as it is for men.

Across the world there are a number of secret societies and organisations, many of which have extensive sub-structures filled with people in senior roles from the police, judiciary, business, religion, education and politics: some are considered to hold insidious influence in government and society. They meet in secret, and membership is only offered to those who have gone through a process of suitability, before an initiation ceremony that involves either fancy dress, trouser leg rolled up, wearing a funny hat, or blindfold: a hitherto unknown handshake may also be required. I can assure you motorcycle training is a simpler more transparent process and a lot of fun.

You may think I've gone off at a tangent, started writing another book, or lost my marbles talking of secret societies, but stay with me because this is an important issue to discuss. I consider them to be ridiculous set ups in a modern, forward thinking world, and in terms of influence in the work place, some will be contravening equality legislation in a range of areas (it would be foolish to underestimate this activity). But the main point I'm making is that they are co-ordinated and operated by men, for men only, with a silly, overblown, testosterone fuelled attitude that screams, 'we know something you don't' (a phrase sometimes uttered by children in school playgrounds). This is either a power-play borne out of insecurity, or an inability to accept or respect women as equals in society. The trap door will open in a millisecond for anyone wishing to disagree with my view; objecting would surely indicate they feel inclined to believe they are a member of an organisation that operates within extreme privacy at best, or is cloaked in complete secrecy at worst; if they are not members of such a group, then there really is nothing to get excited about, is there?

Further, there is an irony missed by misogynistic individuals who, with closed minds and eyes, fail to see the proverbial elephant in the room; those who operate within their secret male only societies, the committee members of male only golf clubs, et al, would not be able to do what they do without women. I am only able to experience the excitement of motorcycling, and life in general, because of my wonderful mum: think about it.

Is it possible these men act the way they do because they really do know the inescapable truth that women have ultimate power and control, and should they ever wish to use it – which they haven't to date, but hold it as a possible silent threat; like a nuclear bomb – would mean we need women more than they need us … an exceptionally good reason for women to believe they should be capable of achieving anything and an indisputable reason, if one was required, why men should treat women with dignity and respect … as we do in the motorcycle fraternity.

As I write, Theresa May has been elected Prime Minister in the UK and has formed a cabinet (a balance of men and women) with minds that can effect positive change, hopefully, and looks less like the old boys' network that had developed under the previous administration … perhaps the revolution has started, or she simply believes – as most of us do in reality – in equality for all.

Now is the right time to share another secret with you … there are in fact two types of learning curve: the male learning curve, and the female learning curve. Although this section is about women in motorcycling, I need to talk about both curves in order to preserve perspective. Guys, do not read pass this point if you have no sense of humour or can't accept contrary to your own belief that the male species does not know *everything* about *everything*.

Both male and female students attend training with the same intention, that is, to gain sufficient competence to ride on the public highway in a safe and effective manner. No problem so far. In fact, during the first modules of compulsory basic training, the initial structured assessment of the process, there is little to choose between the sexes. There are five elements in total that have to be covered.

Element A is an introduction explaining legal paperwork requirements and motorcycle clothing.

Element B is where machine controls are explained and maintenance of bikes is discussed. After the student has been shown how to deal with side and centre stands, they then sit on the bike and turn the engine on and off.

Element C is where the bike starts moving, and there are number of manoeuvres that have to be explained, demonstrated and practised.

Element D is a discussion on the high way code and road riding.

Element E involves a legal minimum (UK and Europe) of two hours riding on the public highway to put everything learned off road into practice. Hopefully, you will be issued with a CBT certificate that lasts for two years until you renew it, or go forward to train and pass the two required UK tests to gain your full motorcycle licence.

It's during element C where the two learning curves become defined. Males initially tend to be more confident, and willing to act on instruction given when first moving off and stopping in a straight line. This confidence continues when asked to start moving around the training ground in either a clockwise or ant-clockwise direction.

However, a motorcycle given momentum will stay up naturally because of physics and it doesn't take long for guys to think they have cracked this biking lark, and you can see their confidence building. Without going into too much detail, and making this book sound like an instructing manual, it stems from an ability to keep their heads up, using their eyes to look and scan around rather than looking down at the controls of the bike, a definite no-no when riding for obvious safety reasons (safe to assume then that drivers who persistently fiddle with smart phones and other in car technology must have a death wish).

I am sure some readers will be associating this 'head up, eyes forward' skill with abilities developed as the hunter-gatherer in cave man times, searching for prey; for food. My view is more simplistic; most initial training sessions usually include males; bravado and the aforementioned testosterone keep the early part of training expeditious.

It is when the required slow riding manoeuvres are introduced that you see the first dip in the male learning curve. It's a truism, from my experience, that everyone can ride quickly in a straight line and stop. Riding slowly using throttle, clutch and rear brake, with due consideration to balance and the centre of gravity is something that requires concentration and practice; it is a major part of riding a motorcycle competently. All students can struggle with this. Getting started is a relatively straight forward process, but it becomes quite apparent at this point to the male student there is a great deal more to learn.

I am not going to give too much detail here, but this ebb and flow is typical throughout the learning process, including and up to the two hour ride out on the road. It shows up again at a later date when the student returns to transfer from the smaller 125cc machine to the larger 650cc bikes for continued training. The problem is we are wired differently. Firstly, I am using the pronoun 'we' because I'm a man, and secondly, as a therapy to acknowledge this affliction of the male gender; that we are given a relatively small amount of information, which, once processed through our grey matter, leads us to believe we are all knowing.

Confused? Men, have you set out on a car journey of some distance (pre-satellite navigation) refusing the map handed to you by the person who really does know that you should study it before leaving, because they know that, 'I know the route,' 'I know where I'm going,' 'I don't need the map,' is rubbish? You still refuse to check the map – out of male pride – when even to a fool it becomes patently obvious you are lost.

The male response is to blame everyone and everything for this predicament; our unreasonable behaviour and uncharitable ranting a reaction to the unpalatable truth that we knew vaguely where we were going, but in reality relying on bucket load of bluff to find our destination; a similar scenario played out in homes around the world when 'man' decides he doesn't need to refer to the IKEA supplied manual when looking at a purchase other than his Swedish meat balls.

I would imagine at this point, the partner in your life is saying, 'That's you! It's just typical of you!'

I understand you may now be cursing me, wishing you hadn't purchased this little book of truth … but really glad you have a satellite navigation app for your smart phone.

Fortunately, my 'bloke' friends who have listened to my philosophy on the male learning curve, have all, sheepishly, put their hands up to admit becoming an expert whilst supping ale at the local pub when we only have the teeniest knowledge of the subject we are professing about. On a graph, the male learning curve would appear jagged, showing the peaks and troughs of first taking in knowledge, and then dipping when realising more learning is evident; a result of boredom with instruction – verbal or written.

On the same graph, the female learning curve is slightly longer over time, but shows a smoother and shallower upward curve as learning takes place. Females absorb instruction avidly, hanging on every word to ensure they have understood what is required. To begin with, they consider moving and balancing on a two-wheeled machine to be more of a magic trick than a technical task involving two pieces of equipment on the handle bar (clutch and throttle). The major problem is, as we have already established, looking down at the controls. I pointed out that unless a naked Brad Pitt (photo of course) was strapped to the petrol tank, perhaps it would be wiser to look ahead.

Again, there may be people who would suggest, going back to cave dwelling days, the woman being the home maker had no use for checking where they were, spatial awareness not high on the list of priorities. I have a more contemporary answer to this too. Despite the best attempts to persuade otherwise, women coming into motorcycling – indeed in many areas of life – feel they are in a man's world, and don't approach it with the same confidence levels as their counterparts, feeling they have more to prove; but the truth is they really haven't. Whilst instructing females, it took a combination of humour; a reminder of the learning process; a clear message there was no rush or time schedule to complete motorcycle training; and a reference to the male learning curve, before they lowered the bar which had been set at an unrealistic height; they then worked steadily and more confidently towards their goal.

A point to be made to all female students is; look at your instructor and consider this … he or she once sat where you now sit: fact. A point to be made to all male students … your instructor will have knowledge that is vital for your progress during the *whole* training process and will require an understanding of why we have two ears and one mouth.

Chapter 8
The Benefits of Motorcycling

- **Confidence**
- **Decision making**
- **Freedom**

The benefits I have experienced over the last 16 years motorcycling have morphed into my life and general wellbeing in such a subtle and subservient way; it seems they arrived without announcement and with no fanfare of exuberant sounding horns or bugles; similar to the way day changes to night; no matter how hard you look, your eyes deceive you when looking for that defining moment of change.

Looking back, I know I have changed. A number of years have passed, giving me perspective to look at the before and after versions of myself, which is a duel edged sword in truth, particularly from an emotional point of view. Some of it is pretty, some not so, and I wouldn't say it's a particularly healthy or cathartic exercise to carry out; it could be easy to find yourself swimming around in a deep pool of regret, or walking around with bruised shins from kicking yourself for not making changes in your life sooner.

Hindsight is an abstract concept and could send us in one of two directions. The second you start thinking about the things you could have done or should have done, is the moment regret could creep in, leading to a downward spiral, talking negatively of wasted years. What we should do is take the positive direction, shrug our shoulders, and consider our experiences as lessons learned, and focus on how we are going to kick start what remains of the life we have in front of us: that is my understanding of the term 'benefit of hindsight'.

Now, let's discuss the reasons why everyone should throw on a leather jacket, become a maverick, ride a motorcycle, and join the revolution. OK, slightly overplayed, but you get the idea.

Confidence

As I mentioned in the introduction, this book is based around experience and I don't profess to be an expert on anything in particular: interestingly, 'experts' balk at the term. They will tell you there is always more to learn. An expert to me is someone who has gained a great deal of knowledge and experience in their chosen field, accepts there is more to discover but, just as importantly, understands where and how to seek out the required information.

On a simplistic level, I believe there is a direct correlation between knowledge and confidence; which in turn increases self-belief and by default, self-esteem. During my motorcycling career, the more I have learned the more comfortable I have become when riding, which in turn increases confidence and consequently the enjoyment factor. Why is this important to know?

Because, amazingly, as adults we forget this is how it works. We approach learning a new skill as if someone has asked us to explain the theory of quantum physics or relativity, literally turning the learning process into rocket science; but all we need to do is muster up the confidence and belief that we can learn a new skill.

In terms of motorcycling, you simply need to trust your instructor and in the training system that has been long established and proven, take in the knowledge and feel your confidence grow as you start to realise that you are truly in total control of the motorcycle. The feeling will be like nothing you have experienced, your adrenalin will be pumping at a great rate of knots and combined with the inevitable dopamine and serotonin hits will give you a feeling of euphoria that may render you speechless. This to me was the point I realised I'd found a release, an antidote if you like, to the confused world I felt I had been drowning in for years.

I have always thought motorcycling akin to chess, albeit with bigger and more exciting pieces – cars, motorbikes, buses and trucks to name a few. As much as your training will focus on technical control and manoeuvres, you will be taught a great deal of what we call road craft, including how to deal with all road, weather and traffic conditions. Again, this is knowledge which we can drop into our tool box of confidence, ready to use when the circumstances dictate.

There is a great deal of information to take in, absorb and act on whilst riding, and to begin with this can be bewildering. However, during your training, particularly as your initial road ride develops, you will find yourself concentrating less on the technical aspect – as it becomes increasingly natural through repetition – and more on your surroundings and what is happening around you. This is where you monitor the other chess pieces, that is, other vehicles around us, but not forgetting pedestrians, animals and cyclists. You need to work out where they are and what they are up to, so you can make informed choices about your next move.

What will become apparent is the confidence you develop when it comes to deciding what you are going to do in a certain situation, but just as importantly being confident in what you are *not* going to do. I call this the discipline switch, as any move should be considered with your safety paramount in any decision. My view is if there is the faintest flicker of doubt in your mind about a decision, then you should err on the side of caution; a mantra I used in training was, 'if you don't know, don't go'. However, once you are comfortable with the controls, you will become more aware of your surroundings and be able relax into your riding, and ultimately look confident to other road users, an aspect of riding not to be underestimated; if it gives you just one more ounce of respect from drivers, who give you time and space, then that's a result.

I have seen students with low levels of confidence and self-esteem change in hours. They may have started training with stooped shoulders or head, but by the end of a day they were smiling and buzzing with excitement, and often, after the road ride had been completed, asked if they could carry on for a while longer. Usually, they went away to consider the next stage of training, fired up by their first riding experience; not realising this new found confidence and energy would start to filter positively into their existing lives in the subtle way it has affected mine.

Decision Making

Confidence and decision making are inextricably and intimately linked. Once self-confidence starts building, it acts like a snowball rolling downhill, gathering momentum and growing in size, eventually becoming big enough to build a snowman. The decision to put a face and scarf on said snowman is both an easy and creative process. This replicates life to a large degree, our decision making becoming positive, quicker and with less procrastination when, through acquired knowledge, our confidence bank, if not bulging, starts to show a healthy deposit.

Motorcycling organises the mind; it has to by default to safety. Every second riding we are taking in information from the 360 degree circle around us, filtering out what is not as important so we can plan for the essential aspects of our ride that are critical, or at least present a higher priority at that moment in time; and this approach is one I now use in every aspect of my life. I decide what I need or want to do, prioritise, and if necessary, drop anything that could hinder the accomplishment of my plan(s).

Before moving on, it is important to discuss a peculiar human need to arrange 'back up' plans which I feel only serve to compound matters. In the past I too often made the mistake of not only developing plan A; but spent time working on a plan B, just to be on the safe side. However, I learned the hard way that this only serves to weaken plan A because we have not spent our mind or resources making it the best plan possible; and suggests that plan B is in place because we are not confident plan A will be successful.

The way around this is to refer back to our first secret that failure is useful. I now put my effort into making plan A the best it can be: if that doesn't work, I learn the lessons and develop a new plan A: I now no longer feel anything I do is second best, and furthermore, it has been instrumental in steering me away from trying to resolve issues with the thinking that caused them in the first place. Emptying the mind of unnecessary clutter will always give us a clearer view of solutions to problems.

We do, however, have to be aware of that sneaky little word called perfection, which evolved from the Latin *perificio* meaning to finish. Even the Greeks, such as Aristotle, couldn't decide on a specific definition, and offered a number of suggestions as to its meaning, such as 'the highest standard of excellence.' In modern parlance that could mean something like 'being the best it can be'. I can accept that and it's as far as I would take the definition for two reasons; to begin with, doing the best we can given a certain set of circumstances, is all we should expect of ourselves. Secondly, if we accept that perfection exists or has been reached, surely that would mean our efforts to learn, question and examine on many levels would be pointless; in which case we may as well put our feet up and drink sangria in the sun all day.

What I am suggesting is never get hung up on what is essentially a word, with wholly subjective connotations, that could leave us demoralised if we took it literally and based our future efforts in work, study or play to attain it: perhaps the words failure and perfection should be consigned to room 101 along with mid-life crisis; just a thought.

Moving on, I refer back to the important decision we sometimes have to make *not* to do something – the discipline switch. In terms of my day to day life, this critical motorcycling necessity has morphed into my psyche, and learning to say 'no' frequently has had, without exaggeration, a life changing effect.

The problem is we all feel the pull, often out of duty or loyalty, to work, friends or family, a combination of these, or to all three. Although I have suggested we do not waste a second of our days, there is a finite limit to what we can achieve in a 24 hour period. However, learning to say no can become a habit that will create space in our mind, and consequently breathing space in our incredibly cluttered lives. 'No' is a small word but has huge potential to make our hour to hour, day to day, week to week existence, easier, relaxing and infinitely more enjoyable; notwithstanding the benefits to our health that follow.

Deciding to say no is not rude or ignorant; in fact the opposite is true. The way we feel overwhelmed with requests for our personal time and effort, is to be blunt (again), our fault. Agreeing to undertake numerous tasks for the family, submitting to every request made for our assistance at work, and taking up every social event on offer, gives the impression that we do have the time and energy to accept it all, forgetting that squeezing a quart into a pint pot is a trick best left to Dynamo – one of the world's greatest illusionists.

Contrary to what you might think, the world will not fall apart if you decide to be honest and make it clear what you can or cannot undertake in a given timescale; what you will find as I have, is that you will be respected for setting the boundaries of your own life, both at work and in the home. If this unfortunately does not prove to be the case for you in the work place, consider your options, keep your self-belief and be confident there will be someone who would appreciate your talents and skills – there would also be the previously mentioned joy notifying HR of your decision to seek pastures new.

Setting, or rather re-booting the boundaries in the home may prove more problematical; especially if your teenager or other half doesn't take kindly to you downing tools in the kitchen or putting clothes or other items left scattered – as if abandoned – in the rubbish bin. Some kind of counselling may well be required, or you could simply contact Bel Mooney (agony aunt at the Daily Mail) who is not at all worried about talking in plain English, and whose advice is always based on good old fashioned common sense. I hesitate to suggest you head for the exit too soon, purely for selfish reasons, as I would not want to be named in divorce proceedings.

Moving swiftly on, what may help in the process of saying no is to take a look at the way we fill in our day planners or diaries. If yours looks anything like mine did, it may resemble a massacre, particularly if you use a red pen to indicate priority; mine looked like a blood bath. So, to begin with, stop using a red pen, it's pointless and furthermore the colour just screams at you like a wailing banshee.

Next, delete entries that clog up the diary such as shopping or dry-cleaning; they serve no purpose except to remind us of the obvious; and the same can be said of 'to do' lists which, simply by looking at them, render us fatigued before we even start the day. There is a smarter way to use 'stick it' notes; if the dry cleaning needs collecting, simply write 'dry cleaning' on a note, slap it on your dashboard and collect it while you're out. Crush your 'to do' lists; you will thank me for it.

So following the motorcycling method of discerning useful information from less useful detail, we can move forward with a clearer path ahead. In terms of our diary entries we have a blank page to look at, unless you have one that splits the days into hours; in which case my suggestion is set fire to it immediately and simply use a blank one to enter times of the meetings you do have – trust me, my logic is sound here, I've done it and proved it keeps the mind calm; I have friends in business who split their working days into a.m. and p.m. only, to avoid 'overcooking' the diary.

Finally, restrict the entries to one, possibly two tasks at the most, but be certain that you can clear them daily, and *always* deal with the most difficult one first. If the task(s) are completed early you have some positive options to consider. You may wish to start a task detailed for the following day, or use the time you have created for some other useful or meaningful purpose.

I'm not being glib or making the process sound easier than it is and I appreciate life's demands would seem less daunting if we were experienced mountain climbers, but as I've hopefully indicated above, once you start identifying what is important and what is not, you will find doing *less* will achieve more than you could imagine. The feeling of completing two tasks in your diary is better than completing two of maybe five tasks that were planned, because you will simply focus on the three uncompleted ones that jump out at you, pointing the finger, proclaiming you are a lightweight at best, and incompetent or a failure at worst.

You can start making firmer decisions today without having ridden a motorcycle, but that would be like going cold turkey when giving up smoking or drinking, and the initial process may be difficult if you think you are letting people down. Shaking that thought is incredibly difficult, but the rewards are tangible and will improve your wellbeing; and far from upsetting people you will find understanding, empathy and even admiration from those around you.

Freedom

Freedom means different things to different people. Freedom to a teenager would mean not washing the dishes or keeping their room tidy (which most don't). To an adult it could be winning the lottery and becoming free from debt; or simply remaining free from illness. In my mind, freedom, in order of priority, sits just below the necessity of air to breath. Most of us are fortunate to live in countries that allow free thought, free speech and free movement; if you think otherwise, imagine yourself in the shoes of a North Korean citizen. Yes, we have rules, regulations and laws, but these are in place to ensure privacy, equality and civility in our society; the responsibilities of freedom we should respect.

Motorcycling is a personal freedom, allowing us to manage the emotional side of life, controlling the unruly elements running riot in the grey matter. Riding is like having a free pass out from the pressures and demands of daily life. It could be an all day trip out to the countryside or coast; it may be just a one hour journey to meet friends for coffee, but the result is the same. Motorcycling creates valuable personal time and space; with no interruption.

Riding is an exclusive activity; you cannot be doing anything else whilst in control of the machine and therefore it squeezes out the chattering matter in your head which is of no consequence whilst riding; colonic irrigation of the mind if you like. I make no apology for the metaphor; many times I have heard people say they have a lot on their mind – although I've heard it put in more earthy terms. I cannot think of a more satisfying freedom than releasing the mental gymnastics that headaches and stress are made up of, starving them of food to survive and cause havoc to mind and body; feeling the rare experience of solitude, being unplugged and off the grid; gaining a true understanding of how it feels to be living in the moment.

Chapter 9
Impossible to Possible

I have made the point that 'can' does not contain the letter 'T' and suggested with appropriate training and application anything is possible; along with the determination that *change* is what you truly desire. I have suggested that success does not come without some failure along the way, but that it should be seen positively as a stepping stone to achievement. Once this principle has been grasped and understood, it acts as the foundation for you to move forward with confidence in anything you do, besides understanding that your life is yours and yours alone to live. If you wake up breathing every day, treat it as a bonus; use every one of those valuable eighty-six thousand four hundred seconds in the most productive way imaginable.

I firmly believe that this world needs those who are content in mind and body and sure of where they are heading; and although they have no control over the wind, are masters at adjusting their sails. It is also vital to understand that we cannot change the world independently, but if we act honestly, compassionately and with conviction, then as a group of individuals we will stand out; and hopefully stand out sufficiently to influence others through our attitude and behaviour.

However, history clearly shows that there are exceptions to the rule. Book shops are filled to the rafters with information regarding individuals who have influenced people, communities, societies and indeed, continents and countries. Gandhi, Mandela, Gorbachev, Churchill, Pankhurst and Bevan, are names straight from my head to paper, and I'm sure you have your own favourites too. The reason for my list is because they all have one thing in common; they made what appeared to be impossible, possible. Magicians and illusionists use deception to achieve the same result, but to give them due credit, even they have to work hard and practice in order for us to ask with disbelief 'how did they do that?'

In retrospect, you could ask the same question of those listed above. The answer lies in all that we have discussed, and in the opening paragraph of this chapter. To sum it up in one sentence and without going into the detailed history of those incredible people on my list, they never gave up, not for one moment; refusing to concede to any physical or emotional barriers that were placed in front of them, deliberately or otherwise, always seeking solutions, believing no issue or problem was impossible to resolve, convinced in their hearts and minds that the impossible was indeed possible.

To put it into perspective, if these influential and determined individuals *had* given up; India may not be the confident independent nation it is today; apartheid may still be the scourge of South Africa; the Cold War may not have come to a close; this book could well have been written in German (from an ironic point of view I hope it will be); we may not have seen the onset of equal rights for women; and we in the UK may not have benefited from the jewel that is the National Health Service.

Finally, there is a group of individuals that I would like to refer to; all of whom have eradicated the word impossible from their mental dictionaries, and serve as an example to us all of what the human mind and body is capable of. I referred earlier to the Rio Olympics of 2016 and the overall success for UK athletics, but I want to you to consider the incredible achievements of over 4000 athletes from 160 nations at the Paralympics. Their levels of performance were, to put it the vernacular, mind blowing and out of this world; particularly when you consider the various disabilities that had to be overcome before a bead of sweat was broken through the extreme and exhausting training process. Feeling humbled is an understatement, because they have to dig so deep for the strength of mind and fortitude that literally sees them to the finishing line; and showing that they too, never know when to give up.

And that is the thought I'd like to leave you with; not guilt or feeling ashamed for realising our lives are, in many cases, more comfortable than others; but believing we have the choice to clear our minds of the litter that serves no useful purpose in our day to day existence and to actively seek opportunities that will enhance our well-being. From the day I sat on a motorcycle and over the many miles covered, I have come to realise that achieving dreams and realising aspirations are well within the reach of everyone; we simply have to let go of anything that hinders or interrupts our efforts and convince ourselves there is no antonym to possible.

In terms of motorcycling, there is no disadvantage to having a disability. If your wish is to give it a go and experience both the freedom and adrenalin rush of riding on two wheels then help and advice is available. The National Association for Bikers with a Disability, based in the UK, has grown to be the world's leading support group for motorcyclists who suffer disability due to accident, illness, genetic conditions or any other causes. They advise on vehicle modifications, control adaptions, vehicle legislation, training matters and legal requirements. Grants are also available (UK only) to cover all or some of the costs involved; so make that call: it may be the missing link for you, too, to make the impossible possible.

Chapter 10
The Motorcycling Fraternity

Society is varied and made up of many types of people and from all backgrounds, some of whom become great friends and others who wouldn't make your birthday card list; those who would drive you to poke your eye out with a cocktail stick rather than become friends. Many people are kind, caring, loving and compassionate; others are cruel, heartless, selfish and arrogant. However, it has been pointed out by many wits that the greatest leveller for us all is death and although extreme, happens to be true.

There have been times when I've become involved with people who seemed to have made it a personal ambition to be annoying and irritating, making life as difficult as possible. I would imagine that you too could come up with a long list of culprits, who, if you had magical powers, you'd turn into a box of your favourite chocolates or snack and eat voraciously; I know I would.

The truth is as we mature, and become less tolerant of chaff, we learn how to avoid these people, or at least ensure they are kept at a safe distance. As I alluded to earlier, we should not allow these individuals to pervade our lives, hanging around like a bad smell or an incessant white noise. If they do start up like a whinging car engine in the winter, belching out carbon monoxide, put an imaginary peg over your nose and close the roller shutter doors in your ears; I do, and it works, but remember not to laugh too much, because all you'll see will be lips moving, like a film with the sound turned down – and it's even funnier if you make up your own dialogue for them while doing it. Failing that, and if the proverbial bullshit is too much to take, do what I do and walk away without saying a word; it's an exquisite response that requires no explanation; but delivers your message like a laser guided missile … with an impact to match.

There is an easier way of course, and that is to only surround ourselves with people who we care about and who in turn care for us. It will require us to use that special word *no*, when making a decision who to allow into our lives and those who we need to keep at the end of a barge pole.

Like me, I'm sure you see the irony in that there are just two times we are all truly equal; the day we are born (in birthday suits) and the day when lights are switched off for the final time. Religion, politics and money contribute significantly to the mire betwixt life and death. As a humanist I am not fooled by the smoke and mirrors of those in positions of control or authority (perceived or otherwise) more because many thrive on the love of power and believe little in the power of love.

The division and angst in society created by said religion, politics, power and money never ceases to disappoint me, but I don't allow it to invade my head space for too long as I wouldn't get out of bed in the morning. I have been described as an idealist because of my views, but if that means being tolerant, gracious and understanding, then I'm guilty as charged. And by the way, I deal with insults by informing the antagonist that whatever they think of me is none of my business; it leaves them disarmed and floundering … words used well have a sharper point than any knife.

Between birth and drawing our last breath, there is usually a very long period called *life* to deal with which brings along all its trials and tribulations. This in turn results in the formulation of hierarchy both at home and in the work place, requiring an adherence to respect, and where due, reverence; the level playing field someway off in the distance that can only be seen through a decent pair of binoculars.

But the good news; there *is* a *living* leveller and I discovered it soon after starting my motorcycle training and before passing my test. Whilst out training most motorcyclists on the road gave a nod of the head when passing. I took this as encouragement for the fact I was training (learner plates being displayed) and also as recognition for joining the motorcycling fraternity. A simple show of appreciation that taps into the human psyche; it makes you feel good for the effort you put into something, whether it be for yourself or someone else. Appreciation of any kind engenders a feeling of being wanted and indicates acceptance, which in turn can add to the motivation you already carry inside.

After I had passed my test, this feature of motorcycling was exemplified during every subsequent mile covered in the UK, Spain and France; the only difference being, in Europe, bikers 'salute' by sticking a leg out. My other discovery was that motorcyclists unknown to each other greet one another with a salutation that would suggest they are close friends and talk as if they are simply continuing a previous conversation. I had not seen or heard anything like it before and cannot think of any other social gathering where the friendship, support and personal interest is as genuine, strong or longer lasting.

At Spirit Rider, I was fortunate to have trained students between 16 and 66 from every conceivable background in terms of work, sex, race, religion and creed; including: apprentices to university students; cleaners to accountants; road-sweepers to solicitors; armed forces personnel to company directors; taxi drivers to airline pilots; vicars to ladies of the night; and nationalities including British, Asian, French, Spanish, Polish, Australian and American: a definitive melting pot of personalities and cultures from which I learned so much and will always be grateful for; and the great thing is they too now know that motorcycling *is* the ultimate therapy.

It is also interesting to note many famous figures across the world, who we all think have got existing amazing and exciting lives, have taken up the challenge of motorcycling. Perhaps it is no coincidence they choose motorcycling as a break from acting, singing, cooking or playing football, and that Keanu Reeves, Ewan McGregor, The Hairy Bikers, David Beckham and others, have themselves also discovered the ultimate therapy.

And this is the point; it doesn't matter who you are, where you're from or what you do, motorcycling is a true living leveller. What motorcyclists across the world realise, is that we all breathe the same air, we all have hearts and minds, we all understand the meaning of respect, and we all have a love of the thrill, excitement and adrenaline rush that riding on two wheels offers; we relegate religion, politics and the foibles of life to talking points for another day … our lives don't get more complicated than that: the simplicity of a veritable fraternity and the ultimate therapy experience, where freedom, friendship and humour will always reign supreme; and the best thing of all? Our club is genuinely inclusive and free to join … so what are you waiting for?

I have referred to individuals who have a lot to say about motorcycles or motorcycling, despite their limited knowledge of either. A small number of these suspects hold stereotypical views of motorcyclists too. In their eyes, we will always be hairy, lairy, and scary Neanderthals, with nothing better to do with our time. Pseudo-experts rarely change their views on much and it isn't worth trying to convince them otherwise, particularly regarding the varied and huge amount of charity work that motorcycle groups undertake. I have gone into detail about those who take up motorcycling and stereotypical is not applicable or relevant; something that will become apparent if you decide to undertake the motorcycle challenge for yourself.

I do hope you'll give it a go and begin a new journey today: but don't forget to nod the head or stick your leg out along the way. It may take baby steps to change your physical or emotional situation at work, at home and in many other areas of your life, but remember, change is only possible if we make a start, bravely taking the first few steps towards a new you … the real you.

There are only two days in the year that nothing can be done. One is called yesterday and the other is called tomorrow. So today is the right day to love, believe, do, and mostly live.

Dalai Lama